Welcome to the study of the book of Ephesians.

I pray God's blessing upon you as you study the material and work through the questions. May He open your mind to receive and understand this information and the strength to live by it.

In Christ

Andrew

Verse by Verse Study of the Book of Ephesians

Copyright Andrew J Lamont-Turner 2012, 2020

First Edition: 2012

Second Edition: 2020

All rights reserved. No part of this publication may be reproduced, distributed, or transmitted in any form or by any means, including photocopying, recording, or other electronic or mechanical methods, without the prior written permission of the author, except in the case of brief quotations embodied in critical reviews and specific other non-commercial uses permitted by copyright law. For permission requests, write to the author, at the email address below. Email: andrew@lamont-turner.co.za

©AJ Lamont-Turner 2012, 2020

Scripture quotations marked CSB have been taken from the Christian Standard Bible®, Copyright © 2017 by Holman Bible Publishers. Used by permission. Christian Standard Bible® and CSB® are federally registered trademarks of Holman Bible Publishers.

Cover Page Design & Photography by

Jess Du Toit Photography

jessejdt@gmail.com

Foreword

No matter how long one studies Scripture, you can never know it all. Every time I read God's Word, I learn something new. I have nothing but awe and wonder at the inspiration of Scripture and how God used the individual personalities of Bible writers to get His ideas and thoughts across, allowing us as His creation, to build a deep relationship with Him. These books I have written, started as a study for myself to gain better knowledge in understanding on how God's Word can touch every aspect of our lives and have a significant impact on how we see and live in the world. Everything we say, do and think, must reflect the knowledge we gain from Scripture. To do this, we must understand Scripture. To understand Scripture, we must be able to feel comfortable with what we read and how we interpret the ancient words. To interpret the ancient words, we will need some guidance. Guidance is what this book and others in the Ancient Words Bible Study Series are. I invite you to read the Bible and go through each verse individually to gain the knowledge you will need to live a life that honours and glories our Saviour, the Lord Jesus Christ.

Contents

FOREWORD 3

CONTENTS 4

INTRODUCTION TO THIS STUDY 6

THE BOOK OF EPHESIANS IN THE BIBLE 8

THE WRITER OF THE BOOK OF EPHESIANS 8

WHEN THE BOOK OF EPHESIANS WAS WRITTEN 9

THE PURPOSE OF WRITING THE BOOK OF EPHESIANS 9

TO WHOM THE BOOK OF EPHESIANS IS WRITTEN 10

BOOK OF EPHESIANS PRACTICALLY APPLIED 10

THE FRAMEWORK OF THE BOOK OF EPHESIANS 17

CONCLUSION 18

SECTION 1: 20

SECTION 2: 22

CHAPTER 1 (READ EPHESIANS CHAPTER 1: 1-23) 22

BOOK OF EPHESIANS, CHAPTER 1: RECAP 32
    ADDITIONAL STUDY QUESTION 1: 33
    ADDITIONAL STUDY QUESTION 2: 33

CHAPTER 2 (READ EPHESIANS CHAPTER 2: 1-20) 34

BOOK OF EPHESIANS, CHAPTER 2: RECAP 41
    ADDITIONAL STUDY QUESTION 1: 41

| ADDITIONAL STUDY QUESTION 2: | 41 |

CHAPTER 3 (READ EPHESIANS CHAPTER 3:1-21) 42

BOOK OF EPHESIANS, CHAPTER 3: RECAP 49

| ADDITIONAL STUDY QUESTION 1: | 49 |
| ADDITIONAL STUDY QUESTION 2: | 49 |

CHAPTER 4 (READ EPHESIANS CHAPTER 4:1-32) 50

BOOK OF EPHESIANS, CHAPTER 4: RECAP 61

| ADDITIONAL STUDY QUESTION 1: | 61 |
| ADDITIONAL STUDY QUESTION 2: | 61 |

CHAPTER 5 (READ EPHESIANS CHAPTER 5:1-33) 62

| ADDITIONAL STUDY QUESTION 1: | 70 |
| ADDITIONAL STUDY QUESTION 2: | 70 |

BOOK OF EPHESIANS, CHAPTER 5: RECAP 70

CHAPTER 6 (READ EPHESIANS CHAPTER 6:1-24) 71

| ADDITIONAL STUDY QUESTION 1: | 79 |
| ADDITIONAL STUDY QUESTION 2: | 79 |

BOOK OF EPHESIANS, CHAPTER 6: RECAP 79

SUMMARY: BOOK OF EPHESIANS: 80

CONGRATULATIONS! 82

ACCEPTING CHRIST AS YOUR SAVIOUR 83

Introduction to this study

This study comprises questions based on the various verses of Scripture taken from the Book of Ephesians.

Section 1 highlights verses from the whole book that draw special attention to specific principles found within the Book of Ephesians.

Section 2 is the verse by verse study that requires the reader to complete the questions and tasks. If this is done in a cell group environment, these answers should be discussed within the group.

Within each section, additional study questions are asked that will require independent study. These questions need careful research and answering.

It is advisable to have a workbook in which to record the answers to the questions. Additional space may also be required to work through the more extended research questions and other tasks that appear throughout the study.

To answer the questions, access to commentary is advisable. However, the actual Bible reading and in many cases, the discussion will also result in in-depth, thoughtful answers.

Answering the questions is not a race. Careful thought should go into writing down the answers and specifically the life application of these questions and their answers.

Engaging in a Bible Study suggests that the reader recognises their need to understand Scripture and the depth of wisdom that follows knowing and understanding God and His ways. This is a spiritual journey and takes time as you investigate the verses, their meaning as the writer intended and their application to life. Ensure prayer precedes each step of the way, allowing the Holy Spirit to guide you, opening your heart and mind to the knowledge of God.

This study matters as it may apply to your life's context. In other words, this study considers the Book's Theology and other principles that are derived from the book within a framework that makes it easier to apply principles to our daily lives.

This study is not a commentary, and although specific information about each book is provided, this study does not engage in textual criticism.

The Book of Ephesians in the Bible

The book of Ephesians is found directly after the book of Galatians and directly before the book of Philippians in the New Testament.

The writer of the Book of Ephesians

The Apostle Paul is the writer if the Book of Ephesians (Ephesians 1:1).

Paul wrote Ephesians, as well as Colossians, Philemon, and Philippians, the other "Prison Epistles," during his first Roman imprisonment, A.D. 60-62 (3:1; 4:1; 6:20; cf. Acts 28:16-31). During this period, he was under house arrest. He lived in his own rented quarters guarded by Roman soldiers.

He was allowed visitors and could minister (Acts 28:16, 30-31). He was not chained in a prison cell as he was during his second Roman imprisonment when he wrote 2 Timothy (cf. 2 Tim. 1:16).

When the Book of Ephesians was Written

With making reference in 2 Timothy 4:12 of sending Tychicus to Ephesus, it would appear that Ephesians was written in Paul's second imprisonment (cf. Ephesians 6:21-22). Some scholars suggest that Ephesians was written at the same time as Colossians due to similarities in the two letters.

The purpose of writing the Book of Ephesians

Paul frequently makes reference to the church and refers to it as a 'mystery' or divine secret. He says this mystery has not been previously revealed. This shows Paul's purpose for writing this letter is to teach about the mystery of the church (Ephesians 1:9; 3:3-4, 9; 5:32; 6:19).

Ephesians focuses on God's planning and provision for salvation in the creation of an organism to which believers belong to affect the ongoing plan for humanities salvation. Also emphasised is the growth of Christians in the knowledge of God and how best to live out one's faith in life, engaging in spiritual warfare. In short, Ephesians explains doctrine and how it can be practically applied to life.

To whom the Book of Ephesians is written

Paul had spent much time in Ephesus (approximately three years; AD 53 to 56 [Acts 19:1 – 20:1]) and knew the church well. He wrote to the congregation in Ephesus with a view to the letter being reads by other churches. It appears Tychicus delivered this letter to the Ephesian church (Eph. 6:21-22).

Book of Ephesians Practically Applied

This book has universal application. The matters Paul deal with Ephesians, have an application to churches in all ages. This is in contrast with 1 Corinthians that deals with the situation in one congregation. In this sense, Ephesians is more like Romans that deal with matters that go far beyond a single sphere. Pauls uses Ephesians to put the place of the church in God's plan, into perspective. Jesus says in Matthew 16:80 … **I will build my church, and the gates of Hades will not overpower it. -- Matthew 16:18 (CSB).** Within Ephesians, Paul brings our attention to the building of the church and the conflict that the church will face. Both these flow from Jesus' statement.

Paul introduces the foundational teaching of Ephesians in the first verse. "To the Saints … in Christ Jesus". These words reflect the make-up of the church and show us what will be covered in the letter. From the name, 'saints', we should understand the diversity and the differences that occur within the church. The words 'in Christ Jesus' points to the unity between individuals within the church. Paul covers the blessing of individuals by God (Ephesians 1:3 – 2:10), the calling of believers to be a part of the church (Ephesians 2:11 – 3:19).

The church is a single organism, created by God by bringing together a diverse selection of individuals with differing characters, backgrounds and personalities (Ephesians 2:11 – 3:19). By using imagery of the human body, Paul explains the various functions of different members of the body with Christ as the controlling Head (Ephesians 2:14-16).

Paul shows in Ephesians first the eternal nature of the church and secondly, the temporal conduct of the church.

Paul explains three things about the nature of the church;

The churches conception. The church has always been a part of God's plan, even before time began. It was not a 'plan B', but was something that was planned and known to God. The church was not something that God had to 'scramble' to put together when the Jews rejected Jesus as Messiah. However, God did not reveal the church in the Old Testament. It was a mystery not revealed until the New Testament. However, it was a part of God's plan from the beginning. This should give us comfort because what God has brought into existence, can never be destroyed by our enemy.

Paul shows us the construction of the church in Ephesians. Paul often draws our attention to God power in Ephesians. Paul prays that his readers will understand the power of God and how this power raised Jesus from the dead (Ephesians 1:18-19). Interestingly, Paul uses four different Greek words when he refers to power (Ephesians 1:19). Resurrection power is the power that raised Jesus from the dead, and this power raises the believer to sit in the heavenly realms with

Christ (Ephesians 2:4-6). This power is available to Christians as they engage the enemy and resist his assaults in trying to break down the church (Ephesians 6:10-11). Christians tend to make less effort because it seems like there is so much against the church. Believers seem to forget that the church is founded through Christ's power and that this power will sustain the church on earth until the time comes for it to be taken up into heaven. In the meantime, believers must use the tools provided and resist the devil and his army.

Paul explains the churches consummation. Paul shows us in Ephesians, how the church will work for God in the future, for all eternity (Ephesians 2:4-7; 3:8-10). God will show through the church, His remarkable Grace to all, forever (Ephesians 2:7). This the church, God's wisdom will also be declared (Ephesians 3:10).

In Ephesians, Paul also wrote about the worldly conduct of the church. The churches eternal nature has a significant impact on its behaviour (Ephesians 4:1).

Unity of the body

Because the church is the body of Christ, individuals must be unified within the body, and this perception is essential in bringing together individuals. The unity between Christian refers to genuine Christians, not those who profess to be Christian.

The church's testimony

Paul encourages the church to live by God's standards and be a testimony to Him (Ephesians 5:15-17). Christians must set aside their lives for God and ensure that they give Him the glory and honour through faithful living. This starts by providing the proper function of relationships. The believer's faith must influence the relationships that exist between people. The church makes a testimony to God through its conduct.

Spiritual warfare

The church is in conflict with forces that oppose God's plans and purposes. Christians must arm themselves and make a stand against these evil spiritual forces (Ephesians 6:10-11).

As genuine Christians, we will heed Paul's words in Ephesians 4:1: **... to walk worthy of the calling you have received -- Ephesians 4:1 (CSB)**

Believers must live their lives, always considering God's eternal plan. In other words, we should live our lives, taking into account God's purposes and will for our lives as members of the body of Christ. God wants us to be Christ-like in our character. In Romans 8:29 Paul writes: **For those he foreknew he also predestined to be conformed to the image of his Son, so that he would be the firstborn among many brothers and sisters. -- Romans 8:29 (CSB).** Furthermore, Paul tells us to speak **the truth in love, let us grow in every way into him who is the head -- Ephesians 4:15 (CSB).** The degree to which we conform is reflected in the way we live our lives. We are to live our lives with God's future plan in mind for our lives. We can do this through regular reading of God's word, prayer, Bible study and regular church attendance.

God can strengthen our ability to walk according to His plans by relying on His power. Paul says: **Now to him who is able to do above and beyond all that we ask or think according to the power that works in us -- Ephesians 3:20 (CSB)**. God allows us access to the power that will allow us to live a worthy life. This is achieved by relying on the Spirit to guide to walk in harmony with God's will. Pau says: **And don't get drunk with wine, which leads to reckless living, but be filled by the Spirit: -- Ephesians 5:18 (CSB).** This means we must always give way to the Holy Spirit, learning to trust His guidance. Paul says something similar in Romans: **And do not offer any parts of it to sin as weapons for unrighteousness. But as those who are alive from the dead, offer yourselves to God, and all the parts of yourselves to God as weapons for righteousness. -- Romans 6:13 (CSB)**

As Christians, our resistance to the devil falls within God's will. Our opposition takes on two aspects. We must be filled with the Spirit, and we must stand firm (Ephesians 6:14). We must always be mindful that our enemies are not other people, but spiritual beings and forces. We have spiritual weapons to resist our spiritual enemies (Ephesians 6:14-18).

The church is created through Christ and by Christ. The church is there to make a difference in the lives of people and its members. To make a difference, the church must be different. If the church conforms to the world, then it can't challenge the world. It must be holy and advocate holy living. Its members living faithful lives that reflect God's character, giving Him honour and glory by being a living testimony to Him. Through Ephesians, we learn that to be able to help people, we must deal with issues of unity, love, holiness and prayer.

The church and its members must remember their position in Christ and resist becoming a part of this world and its desires. Prayer is the church's most powerful weapon and should be relied upon more than picketing or politics. It is when the church fully understands its purpose that it can be most effective.

The framework of the Book of Ephesians

Books of the Bible have frameworks within which we can understand the way the author has tried to get their message across. This is like the table of contents in our own writing. However, ancient writers did not have these table of contents in their writing, so we develop these frameworks to help us see the structure of the written word and help us make sense of the message. By getting a bigger picture of the book being studied, it helps us understand why certain things have been said at various places in the book. It helps us get a better understanding of the "flow" of the book.

I.   Greeting 1:1-2

II.   The Christian's calling 1:3—3:21
     A. Individual calling 1:3—2:10
          1.   God's Richest Blessings 1:3-14

      2.   God's Power in Christ 1:15-23
      3.   From Death to Life 2:1-10
  B. Corporate calling 2:11-3:19
      1.   Unity in Christ 2:11-22
      2.   Paul's Ministry to the Gentiles 3:1-13
      3.   Prayer for Spiritual Power 3:14-19
  C.   Doxology 3:20-21

III.   The Christian's conduct 4:1—6:20
  A. Spiritual walk 4:1—6:9
      1.   Unity and Diversity in the Body of Christ 4:1-16
      2.   Living the New Life 4:17-32
      3.   Walking in love 5:1-6
      4.   Light versus Darkness 5:7-14
      5.   Consistency in the Christian Lifestyle 5:15—6:9
  B. Christian warfare 6:10-20

IV. Conclusion 6:21-24

Conclusion

Ephesians shows us that the church is a planned part of God's plan, growing through Christ's power, impacting on believer's lives and enables them to resist God's enemy.

This letter was meant for circulation among other churches besides Ephesus. In this letter, Paul draws attention to the supremacy of Christ. He provides information on both the nature of the church and on how church members should live. Besides this, he stresses the unity of all believers regardless of sex, nationality, or social rank. In the home and the church, living the Christian life can be difficult because we can't hide our imperfections from those who know us well. Close relationships between flawed people may lead to friction. On the other hand, these relationships may also lead to increased faith and deepened dependence on God. We can build unity in our churches through willing submission to Christ's leadership and heart-felt service to each another.

SECTION 1:

Give careful thought about these verses below. Write down your own ideas about and what the highlighted verses mean to you or how you understand what Paul is trying to teach you.

Blessed is the God and Father of our Lord Jesus Christ, who has blessed us with every spiritual blessing in the heavens in Christ. -- Ephesians 1:3 (CSB)

He exercised this power in Christ by raising him from the dead and seating him at his right hand in the heavens — far above every ruler and authority, power and dominion, and every title given, not only in this age but also in the one to come. -- Ephesians 1:20-21 (CSB)

Then we will no longer be little children, tossed by the waves and blown around by every wind of teaching, by human cunning with cleverness in the techniques of deceit. -- Ephesians 4:14 (CSB)

Pay careful attention, then, to how you walk — not as unwise people but as wise — 16 making the most of the time, because the days are evil. -- Ephesians 5:15-16 (CSB)

SECTION 2:

Chapter 1 (READ Ephesians Chapter 1: 1-23)

Paul, an apostle of Christ Jesus by God's will: To the faithful saints in Christ Jesus at Ephesus. ² Grace to you and peace from God our Father and the Lord Jesus Christ. -- Ephesians 1:1-2 (CSB)

Why do you think does Paul say "by God's will?

> **Did you know:**
>
> By the writing of the letter to the Ephesians, Paul had been a Christian for nearly 30 years. He had taken three missionary trips and established churches all around the Mediterranean Sea.

> **Interesting:**
>
> Ephesus was a major city in the Roman Empire, as well as Rome, Corinth, Antioch, and Alexandria. Paul first visited Ephesus on his second missionary journey (Acts 18:19-21). On his third missionary journey, Paul stayed there for almost three years (Acts 19). He later met with the elders of the Ephesian church at Miletus (Acts 20:16-38). Ephesus was a commercial, political, and religious centre for all of Asia Minor. The temple to the Greek goddess Artemis (Diana is her Roman equivalent) was located there.

"Faithful saints in Christ Jesus"—what an excellent reputation! Such a label would be an honour for any believer. What would it take for others to characterize you as a faithful follower of Christ Jesus?

³ Blessed is the God and Father of our Lord Jesus Christ, who has blessed us with every spiritual blessing in the heavens in Christ. -- Ephesians 1:3 (CSB)

What does "who has blessed us with every spiritual blessing in the heavens" mean?

⁴ For he chose us in him, before the foundation of the world, to be holy and blameless in love before him. -- Ephesians 1:3-4 (CSB)

What do you think, does Paul mean he says that God chose us?

What part does Jesus have in this process?

⁵ He predestined us to be adopted as sons through Jesus Christ for himself, according to the good pleasure of his will, ⁶ to the praise of his glorious grace that he lavished on us in the Beloved One. -- Ephesians 1:5-6 (CSB)

Explain what you think is meant with the use of the word 'predestined'.

Read Romans 8:17. What picture does Romans 8:17 and Ephesians 1:5 create about our relationship with God?

> **Did you know:**
>
> **Under Roman law, adopted children possessed the same rights and privileges as biological children, even if they had been slaves. Paul uses this concept to demonstrate how intimate our relationship to God is.**

Would you consider yourself adopted by God?

---

7 In him we have redemption through his blood, the forgiveness of our trespasses, according to the riches of his grace 8 that he richly poured out on us with all wisdom and understanding. -- Ephesians 1:7-8 (CSB)

Explain what is meant by 'redemption through His blood'.

> **Did you know:**
>
> **Forgiveness** was granted in Old Testament times based on the shedding of animals' blood (Leviticus 17:11). Now we are forgiven based on the shedding of Jesus' blood—he died as the perfect and final sacrifice.

What does the word 'grace' mean?

9 He made known to us the mystery of his will, according to his good pleasure that he purposed in Christ 10 as a plan for the right time — to bring everything together in Christ, both things in heaven and things on earth in him. -- Ephesians 1:9-10 (CSB)

What is the 'mystery'?

Why do you think, did God not reveal this 'mystery' in the Old Testament?

[11] In him we have also received an inheritance, because we were predestined according to the plan of the one who works out everything in agreement with the purpose of his will, [12] so that we who had already put our hope in Christ might bring praise to his glory. -- Ephesians 1:11-12 (CSB)

What is the inheritance we have received?

[13] In him you also were sealed with the promised Holy Spirit when you heard the word of truth, the gospel of your salvation, and when you believed. [14] The Holy Spirit is the down payment of our inheritance, until the redemption of the possession, to the praise of his glory. -- Ephesians 1:13-14 (CSB)

What do you think, does Paul mean in verses 13 and 14?

¹⁵ This is why, since I heard about your faith in the Lord Jesus and your love for all the saints, ¹⁶ I never stop giving thanks for you as I remember you in my prayers. ¹⁷ I pray that the God of our Lord Jesus Christ, the glorious Father, would give you the Spirit of wisdom and revelation in the knowledge of him. -- Ephesians 1:15-17 (CSB)

What does verse 15 tell you about the believers in Ephesus?

What attitude does Paul emphasise in verse 16?

What do we learn about prayer in verse 17?

What point does Paul make about knowledge in verse 17?

Paul prayed for believers to know God better. How do we get to know someone?

Do you really know God, or do you just know about him?

[18] I pray that the eyes of your heart may be enlightened so that you may know what is the hope of his calling, what is the wealth of his glorious inheritance in the saints, [19] and what is the immeasurable greatness of his power toward us who believe, according to the mighty working of his strength. [20] He exercised this power in Christ by raising him from the dead and seating him at his right hand in the heavens -- Ephesians 1:18-20 (CSB)

What does verses 18 to 20 tell you about God's power?

What was the ultimate manifestation of God's power, according to verse 20?

Where is Christ now seated?

> **Prayer suggestion:**
>
> Paul says, in Romans 8:37-39, that nothing can separate us from God and his love. Thank you, Father, that your love holds us secure forever.

²¹ far above every ruler and authority, power and dominion, and every title given, not only in this age but also in the one to come. ²² And he subjected everything under his feet and appointed him as head over everything for the church, ²³ which is his body, the fullness of the one who fills all things in every way. -- Ephesians 1:21-23 (CSB)

What is the extent of Christ's power?

> **Did you know:**
>
> **Christ is the head, and we are the body of his church. Paul uses this metaphor in Romans 12:4-5; 1Corinthians 12:12-27; and Colossians 3:15 as well as throughout the book of Ephesians.**

What does the image of the body show?

How do these verses strengthen your faith?

Book of Ephesians, Chapter 1: Recap

What would you say is the main point Paul is trying to make in Chapter 1 of Ephesians?

Summarize the points that stand out most to you in this chapter of Ephesians.

How have these points made you reflect on your own life?

> **Prayer Suggestion:**
>
> **Dear Lord. You have opened my eyes with Scripture, and there some things I would like to change. Please give me the wisdom to know where I need to change and the courage to bring about these changes.**

Additional Study Question 1:

How many references to the heaven realms do we find in Ephesians? List them.

Additional Study Question 2:

Read the following verses: Romans 5:9; Ephesians 2:13; Colossians 1:20; Hebrews 9:22; 1 Peter 1:19). What do they tell us about Jesus as a sacrifice?

Chapter 2 (READ Ephesians Chapter 2: 1-20)

And you were dead in your trespasses and sins ² in which you previously walked according to the ways of this world, according to the ruler of the power of the air, the spirit now working in the disobedient. -- Ephesians 2:1-2 (CSB)

Of what is Paul reminding his readers in verse 1?

Who is Paul referring to in verse 2?

³ We too all previously lived among them in our fleshly desires, carrying out the inclinations of our flesh and thoughts, and we were by nature children under wrath as the others were also. -- Ephesians 2:3 (CSB)

What does Paul say about the nature of humanity?

What does Paul mean with the words 'children under wrath'?

⁴ But God, who is rich in mercy, because of his great love that he had for us, ⁵ made us alive with Christ even though we were dead in trespasses. You are saved by grace! -- Ephesians 2:4-5 (CSB)

What did God's mercy result in?

Does this mercy mean we will no longer sin?

> **Did you know:**
>
> **Through faith in Christ, we stand acquitted before God (Romans 3:21-22).**

What does it mean that we are 'alive in Christ'?

Do you consider yourself alive in Christ?

⁶ He also raised us up with him and seated us with him in the heavens in Christ Jesus, ⁷ so that in the coming ages he might display the immeasurable riches of his grace through his kindness to us in Christ Jesus. -- Ephesians 2:6-7 **(CSB)**

Explain what Paul is saying in verses 6 and 7.

⁸ For you are saved by grace through faith, and this is not from yourselves; it is God's gift — ⁹ not from works, so that no one can boast. -- Ephesians 2:8-9 (CSB)

Does verse 8 mean that we can earn our salvation?

Can our works give us an opportunity for salvation?

¹⁰ For we are his workmanship, created in Christ Jesus for good works, which God prepared ahead of time for us to do. -- Ephesians 2:10 (CSB)

In verses 8-9, it seems that we can't work for our salvation, however, in verse 10 its says that we are prepared for good works. Explain this apparent contradiction.

11 So, then, remember that at one time you were Gentiles in the flesh — called "the uncircumcised" by those called "the circumcised," which is done in the flesh by human hands. 12 At that time you were without Christ, excluded from the citizenship of Israel, and foreigners to the covenants of promise, without hope and without God in the world. 13 But now in Christ Jesus, you who were far away have been brought near by the blood of Christ. -- Ephesians 2:11-13 (CSB)

Who are 'the uncircumcised' and the 'circumcised'?

Have you ever felt separate, excluded, hopeless?

> **Did you know:**
>
> Spiritual pride stops us from being honest with ourselves about our own faults while focusing on the mistakes of others. Don't be proud of your salvation. Be humble and thank God for what He has done. Encourage others who might be struggling in their faith.

¹⁴ For he is our peace, who made both groups one and tore down the dividing wall of hostility. In his flesh, ¹⁵ he made of no effect the law consisting of commands and expressed in regulations, so that he might create in himself one new man from the two, resulting in peace. -- **Ephesians 2:14-15 (CSB)**

List at three barriers people can build up between themselves.

Who breaks down these barriers?

What do you think, should the focus of unity in the body of Christ?

What does it mean that Christ created 'one new man out of two'?

Would you say the church lives up to this expectation? Why? Why not?

16 He did this so that he might reconcile both to God in one body through the cross by which he put the hostility to death. 17 He came and proclaimed the good news of peace to you who were far away and peace to those who were near. 18 For through him we both have access in one Spirit to the Father. -- Ephesians 2:16-18 (CSB)

How did Christ put the hostility to death?

Who is the Spirit referred to in verse 18?

¹⁹ So, then, you are no longer foreigners and strangers, but fellow citizens with the saints, and members of God's household, ²⁰ built on the foundation of the apostles and prophets, with Christ Jesus himself as the cornerstone. ²¹ In him the whole building, being put together, grows into a holy temple in the Lord. ²² In him you are also being built together for God's dwelling in the Spirit. -- Ephesians 2:19-22 (CSB)

When you read verses 19 to 20, do you get the idea that the church is a building or people? Why do you say so?

What does it mean to be built on the foundation of the apostles and prophets?

Book of Ephesians, Chapter 2: Recap

What would you say is the main point Paul is trying to make in Chapter 2 of Ephesians?

Summarize the points that stand out most to you in this chapter of Ephesians.

How have these points made you reflect on your own life?

Additional Study Question 1:

Look at Ephesians 2:14; 16; 18; 19 and 20-21. In what ways has reconciliation taken place?

Additional Study Question 2:

Read 1 Corinthians 15:2-23. What is the Apostle Paul talking about here? How does our position in Christ secure this outcome?

Chapter 3 (READ Ephesians Chapter 3:1-21)

For this reason, I, Paul, the prisoner of Christ Jesus on behalf of you Gentiles — -- Ephesians 3:1 (CSB)

Explain why Paul says he is a 'prisoner of Christ Jesus on behalf of you Gentiles'.

Do circumstances make you wonder if God has lost control of this world?

² assuming you have heard about, haven't you, about the administration of God's grace that he gave me for you? ³ The mystery was made known to me by revelation, as I have briefly written above. -- Ephesians 3:2-3 (CSB)

What administration was Paul given?

What mystery is Paul referring to?

⁴ By reading this you are able to understand my insight into the mystery of Christ. ⁵ This was not made known to people in other generations as it is now revealed to his holy apostles and prophets by the Spirit: ⁶ The Gentiles are coheirs, members of the same body, and partners in the promise in Christ Jesus through the gospel. -- Ephesians 3:4-6 (CSB)

To whom is the mystery now revealed?

Explain what is meant by the mystery.

> **Did you know:**
>
> **We are told in the Old Testament that the Gentiles would receive salvation (Isaiah 49:6). The mystery was never revealed in the Old Testament that all Gentile and Jewish believers would become equal in the body of Christ. This equality was accomplished when Jesus destroyed the barrier of hostility and created a new unified people (Ephesians 2:14-15).**

⁷ I was made a servant of this gospel by the gift of God's grace that was given to me by the working of his power. -- Ephesians 3:7 (CSB)

What does Paul mean by saying he is a 'servant of the gospel'?

How was the gift given?

What do you think he means by saying this?

⁸ This grace was given to me — the least of all the saints — to proclaim to the Gentiles the incalculable riches of Christ, -- Ephesians 3:8 (CSB)

Did Paul have a specific people he had to approach with the gospel?

Do you feel like you are not qualified to do God's work?

Can you draw some encouragement from what Paul says in verse 8?

⁹ and to shed light for all about the administration of the mystery hidden for ages in God who created all things. ¹⁰ This is so that God's multi-faceted wisdom may now be made known through the church to the rulers and authorities in the heavens. -- Ephesians 3:9-10 (CSB)

What does Paul say he has to do in verse 9?

What do you think Paul means in verse 10?

¹¹ This is according to his eternal purpose accomplished in Christ Jesus our Lord. ¹² In him we have boldness and confident access through faith in him. -- Ephesians 3:11-12 (CSB)

What is God's eternal purpose?

How was it accomplished in Christ Jesus?

¹³ So, then, I ask you not to be discouraged over my afflictions on your behalf, for they are your glory. -- Ephesians 3:13 (CSB)

Why should Paul's suffering make the Ephesians feel honoured?

¹⁴ For this reason I kneel before the Father ¹⁵ from whom every family in heaven and on earth is named. -- Ephesians 3:14-15 (CSB)

Explain who or what Paul is referring to as a family.

¹⁶ I pray that he may grant you, according to the riches of his glory, to be strengthened with power in your inner being through his Spirit, ¹⁷ and that Christ may dwell in your hearts through faith. I pray that you, being rooted and firmly established in love, ¹⁸ may be able to comprehend with all the saints what is the length and width, height and depth of God's love, ¹⁹ and to know Christ's love that surpasses knowledge, so that you may be filled with all the fullness of God. -- Ephesians 3:16-19 (CSB)

Explain to what extent Paul says God loves us?

What do you think, Paul means by referring to the fullness of God?

²⁰ Now to him who is able to do above and beyond all that we ask or think according to the power that works in us — ²¹ to him be glory in the church and in Christ Jesus to all generations, forever and ever. Amen. -- Ephesians 3:20-21 (CSB)

> **Did you Know:**
>
> This prayer (verses 20 and 21) of praise to God ends part 1 of Ephesians. In the first section, Paul describes the role of the church. In part 2 (chapters 4-6), he explains how church members should live according to God's standards. Paul first lays a foundation of doctrine and then practically applies the truth he has laid down.

Book of Ephesians, Chapter 3: Recap

What would you say is the main point Paul is trying to make in Chapter 3 of Ephesians?

Summarize the points that stand out most to you in this chapter of Ephesians.

How have these points made you reflect on your own life?

Additional Study Question 1:

Read Acts 9. Write down a blow by blow account of what transpired in chapter 9 of Acts.

Additional Study Question 2:

Read Matthew 16:24. How does what Christ asks of us, compares to what Paul says in verse 13 of chapter 3? Do you think you could suffer for your beliefs?

Chapter 4 (READ Ephesians Chapter 4:1-32)

Therefore I, the prisoner in the Lord, urge you to walk worthy of the calling you have received, ² with all humility and gentleness, with patience, bearing with one another in love, -- Ephesians 4:1-2 (CSB)

What does Paul mean when he challenges believers to 'walk worthy of the calling'?

Can people see Christ in you? How well do you represent Him?

Explain, using Paul's words in verse 2, how believers should act towards each other.

³ making every effort to keep the unity of the Spirit through the bond of peace. -- Ephesians 4:3 (CSB)

Spirit is spelt with a capital letter. Who is the Spirit Paul is referring to?

⁴ There is one body and one Spirit — just as you were called to one hope at your calling — ⁵ one Lord, one faith, one baptism, ⁶ one God and Father of all, who is above all and through all and in all. ⁷ Now grace was given to each one of us according to the measure of Christ's gift. -- Ephesians 4:4-7 (CSB)

List the seven aspects of our calling, as expressed by Paul.

Paul talks about a gift given by Christ. What do you think this refers to?

What do you think Paul means when referring to God the Father and says He is 'above all, through all and in all'?

⁸ For it says: When he ascended on high, he took the captives captive; he gave gifts to people. -- Ephesians 4:8 (CSB)

Verse 8 quotes Psalm 68:18. Can you relate this to what Christ has done for believers? How?

⁹ But what does "he ascended" mean except that he also descended to the lower parts of the earth? -- Ephesians 4:9 (CSB)

What does 'descended to the lower parts of the earth' mean?

¹⁰ The one who descended is also the one who ascended far above all the heavens, to fill all things. ¹¹ And he himself gave some to be apostles, some prophets, some evangelists, some pastors and teachers, ¹² to equip the saints for the work of ministry, to build up the body of Christ, -- Ephesians 4:10-12 (CSB)

Who is Paul talking about in verse 10?

What is being given in verse 11?

What was the purpose of these things that were given?

What do you think, Christ has given you to work within His church? Why?

¹³ until we all reach unity in the faith and in the knowledge of God's Son, growing into maturity with a stature measured by Christ's fullness. -- Ephesians 4:13 (CSB)

How do you feel about being a part of the body of Christ?

Do you think that the body can accomplish more than the sum of its parts? Why?

¹⁴ Then we will no longer be little children, tossed by the waves and blown around by every wind of teaching, by human cunning with cleverness in the techniques of deceit. -- Ephesians 4:14 (CSB)

What do you think Paul means in verse 14?

15 But speaking the truth in love, let us grow in every way into him who is the head — Christ. 16 From him the whole body, fitted and knit together by every supporting ligament, promotes the growth of the body for building itself up in love by the proper working of each individual part. -- Ephesians 4:15-16 (CSB)

What does Paul say, is a mark of a mature Christian in verse 15?

How can we grow to be Christ-like?

As part of Christ's body, do you reflect part of Christ's character and carry out your unique role in his work?

Prayer Suggestion:

Pray and ask God to give you the wisdom and strength to live your life in such a way to reflect Jesus' character in your own life.

¹⁷ Therefore, I say this and testify in the Lord: You should no longer walk as the Gentiles do, in the futility of their thoughts. ¹⁸ They are darkened in their understanding, excluded from the life of God, because of the ignorance that is in them and because of the hardness of their hearts. ¹⁹ They became callous and gave themselves over to promiscuity for the practice of every kind of impurity with a desire for more and more. -- Ephesians 4:17-19 (CSB)

What does Paul mean with 'in the futility of their thoughts'?

Where do you think the ignorance of the gentiles comes from?

What personality trait can 'hardness in their hearts' be compared to?

What do you think, the 'desire for more and more' means?

[20] But that is not how you came to know Christ, [21] assuming you heard about him and were taught by him, as the truth is in Jesus, [22] to take off your former way of life, the old self that is corrupted by deceitful desires, [23] to be renewed in the spirit of your minds, [24] and to put on the new self, the one created according to God's likeness in righteousness and purity of the truth. -- Ephesians 4:20-24 (CSB)

Do you think people should be able to tell the difference between Christians and non-Christians? Why?

What does Paul mean about taking off 'your former life'?

Explain what according to Paul, the 'new likeness' is like?

As you consider the past year, have your thoughts, attitudes, and actions changed at all?

---

²⁵ Therefore, putting away lying, speak the truth, each one to his neighbor, because we are members of one another. -- Ephesians 4:25 (CSB)

What does Paul say we should replace lying with?

Who is our neighbour?

Why, according to Paul, should we be good to each another?

---

²⁶ Be angry and do not sin. Don't let the sun go down on your anger, ²⁷ and don't give the devil an opportunity. -- Ephesians 4:26-27 (CSB)

What do you think Paul means when he says we can be angry, but not sin?

Why would the devil be given an opportunity if we are angry?

Are you presently angry with someone? What steps can you take to resolve your conflict?

What is the principle about a conflict that Paul emphasises in verse 26?

> **Prayer Suggestion:**
>
> **Pray and ask God to allow you to find it within your heart to make peace with someone who has harmed or offended you. Pray for wisdom to show grace toward that other person.**

²⁸ Let the thief no longer steal. Instead, he is to do honest work with his own hands, so that he has something to share with anyone in need. ²⁹ No foul language should come from your mouth, but only what is good for building up someone in need, so that it gives grace to those who hear. -- Ephesians 4:28-29 (CSB)

What principle is Paul talking about in verse 28?

What type of language should be coming out of our mouths, according to verse 29?

What should the result of this type of language be?

> **30 And don't grieve God's Holy Spirit. You were sealed by him for the day of redemption. 31 Let all bitterness, anger and wrath, shouting and slander be removed from you, along with all malice. 32 And be kind and compassionate to one another, forgiving one another, just as God also forgave you in Christ. -- Ephesians 4:30-32 (CSB)**

What is the purpose of being sealed?

How do you think, could we change and remove these aspects of our character in verse 31?

What godly personality traits should we emphasise in our lifestyles, according to verse 32?

Why should we do this?

Do you think our own forgiveness is dependent on our forgiving others?

Book of Ephesians, Chapter 4: Recap

What would you say is the main point Paul is trying to make in Chapter 4 of Ephesians?

Summarize the points that stand out most to you in this chapter of Ephesians.

How have these points made you reflect on your own life?

Additional Study Question 1:

Read 1 Corinthians 12:12-13. What are the seven aspects of our faith that should unite believers? Do you agree? Explain your agreement or disagreement.

Additional Study Question 2:

Read John 3:6; Act 1:5; and Ephesians 1:13-14. From these verses, can you write down what some of the things are, that the Holy Spirit impacts?

Chapter 5 (READ Ephesians Chapter 5:1-33)

Therefore, be imitators of God, as dearly loved children, ² and walk in love, as Christ also loved us and gave himself for us, a sacrificial and fragrant offering to God. -- Ephesians 5:1-2 (CSB)

What does Paul say we should do in verse 1?

How do you think one can walk in love? What does this mean to us as individuals?

Why do you think, would Christ's sacrifice have been a 'fragrant offering'?

³ But sexual immorality and any impurity or greed should not even be heard of among you, as is proper for saints. ⁴ Obscene and foolish talking or crude joking are not suitable, but rather giving thanks. -- Ephesians 5:3-4 (CSB)

What does Paul say, the Christian's life should be free from?

What does Paul say we should be doing instead of 'foolish talking'?

Do you think we can we praise God and remind others of his goodness when we are speaking coarsely?

⁵ For know and recognize this: Every sexually immoral or impure or greedy person, who is an idolater, does not have an inheritance in the kingdom of Christ and of God. ⁶ Let no one deceive you with empty arguments, for God's wrath is coming on the disobedient because of these things. ⁷ Therefore, do not become their partners. -- Ephesians 5:5-7 (CSB)

What do you think is the point Paul is making in verse 5?

What does Paul caution us within verse 6? What are some empty arguments that we hear in the world today?

How can we stop ourselves from falling for empty arguments?

⁸ For you were once darkness, but now you are light in the Lord. Walk as children of light — ⁹ for the fruit of the light consists of all goodness, righteousness, and truth — -- Ephesians 5:8-9 (CSB)

What does it mean to have been 'darkness' and now 'light'?

What does the fruit of the light consist of?

¹⁰ testing what is pleasing to the Lord. ¹¹ Don't participate in the fruitless works of darkness, but instead expose them. ¹² For it is shameful even to mention what is done by them in secret. ¹³ Everything exposed by the light is made visible, -- Ephesians 5:10-13 (CSB)

Why do you think, does Paul admonish Christians not to remain silent about something bad they know of?

¹⁴ for what makes everything visible is light. Therefore it is said: Get up, sleeper, and rise up from the dead, and Christ will shine on you. -- Ephesians 5:14 (CSB)

Verse 14 is not a quote from the Bible. It may have been a hymn that the Ephesians were familiar with. What do you think is the point that Paul is making?

¹⁵ Pay careful attention, then, to how you walk — not as unwise people but as wise — ¹⁶ making the most of the time, because the days are evil. -- Ephesians 5:15-16 (CSB)

What are some of the things believers can do to ensure that they pay careful attention to how they 'walk'?

What is Paul encouraging believers to do in verse 16?

¹⁷ So don't be foolish, but understand what the Lord's will is. ¹⁸ And don't get drunk with wine, which leads to reckless living, but be filled by the Spirit: ¹⁹ speaking to one another in psalms, hymns, and spiritual songs, singing and making music with your heart to the Lord, -- Ephesians 5:17-19 (CSB)

How can we know what the Lord's will is?

What are the three things that result from a Spirit-filled life?

What is the difference between being filled with the Spirit and being filled with wine? Name two differences.

> **Prayer suggestion:**
>
> **Submit yourself to His leading and continuously draw on his power to live a God-honouring life.**

[20] giving thanks always for everything to God the Father in the name of our Lord Jesus Christ, [21] submitting to one another in the fear of Christ. -- Ephesians 5:20-21 (CSB)

What attitude does Paul say we should always have?

What does it mean to submit to each other?

[22] Wives, submit to your husbands as to the Lord, [23] because the husband is the head of the wife as Christ is the head of the church. He is the Savior of the body. [24] Now as the church submits to Christ, so also wives are to submit to their husbands in everything. -- Ephesians 5:22-24 (CSB)

Explain what Biblical submission is and how it might be different from worldly submission.

Why did Paul tell wives to submit and husbands to love?

²⁵ Husbands, love your wives, just as Christ loved the church and gave himself for her ²⁶ to make her holy, cleansing her with the washing of water by the word. ²⁷ He did this to present the church to himself in splendor, without spot or wrinkle or anything like that, but holy and blameless. ²⁸ In the same way, husbands are to love their wives as their own bodies. He who loves his wife loves himself. -- Ephesians 5:25-28 (CSB)

How does Paul relate the relationship between a husband and wife, to that of Christ and the church?

> **Did you know:**
>
> **Paul applies twice as many words to calling husbands to love their wives as opposed to encouraging wives to submit to their husbands.**

How does Paul say, should a man love his wife?

What does Christ's death do for the church?

---

²⁹ For no one ever hates his own flesh but provides and cares for it, just as Christ does for the church, ³⁰ since we are members of his body. ³¹ For this reason a man will leave his father and mother and be joined to his wife, and the two will become one flesh. -- Ephesians 5:29-31 (CSB)

What does Paul teach about depth or marriage?

---

³² This mystery is profound, but I am talking about Christ and the church. ³³ To sum up, each one of you is to love his wife as himself, and the wife is to respect her husband. -- Ephesians 5:32-33 (CSB)

How does this depth of the relationship between husband and wife apply to the church?

Additional Study Question 1:

Read Matthew 5:15-16. What principle from the Sermon on the Mount does Jesus stress?

Additional Study Question 2:

In verse 14 of chapter 5, Paul quotes from a hymn. The hymn seems to have been based on Isaiah 26:19; Isaiah 51:17; Isaiah 52:1; Isaiah 60:1; and Malachi 4:2. Read these verses and summarise what you think they mean.

Book of Ephesians, Chapter 5: Recap

What would you say is the main point Paul is trying to make in Chapter 5 of Ephesians?

Summarize the points that stand out most to you in this chapter of Ephesians.

How have these points made you reflect on your own life?

Chapter 6 (READ Ephesians Chapter 6:1-24)

Children, obey your parents in the Lord, because this is right. ² Honor your father and mother, which is the first commandment with a promise, ³ so that it may go well with you and that you may have a long life in the land. -- Ephesians 6:1-3 (CSB)

Do you think there is a difference between obeying your parents and honouring them?

How do you think, does this honouring lead to a long life?

⁴ Fathers, don't stir up anger in your children, but bring them up in the training and instruction of the Lord. -- Ephesians 6:4 (CSB)

How would one bring children up in the 'training and instruction of the Lord'?

Did you know:

Many communities honour their elders. They respect the elders' wisdom, accede to their authority, and provide for their comfort and contentment. Christians should act in this way.

Interesting:

Parental discipline must help children grow. Parents should not exasperate and provoke their children to anger or discouragement (Colossians 3:21). Being a parent is not easy. Raising children takes large amounts of patience. Frustration and anger should not be the underlying reason to discipline. Parents must act in love, considering their children as Jesus acted toward the people he loves. This is essential to help children's development and their understanding of Christ is and what He is like.

⁵ **Slaves, obey your human masters with fear and trembling, in the sincerity of your heart, as you would Christ. -- Ephesians 6:5 (CSB)**

Why do you think, did Paul have to deal with the relationship between masters and their slaves?

> **Did you know:**
>
> **In Paul's time, women, children, and slaves had virtually no rights. However, in the church, they were allowed freedoms that they were denied in society. Paul strongly encourages husbands, parents, and masters to be caring.**

⁶ **Don't work only while being watched, as people-pleasers, but as slaves of Christ, do God's will from your heart. ⁷ Serve with a good attitude, as to the Lord and not to people, ⁸ knowing that whatever good each one does, slave or free, he will receive this back from the Lord. -- Ephesians 6:6-8 (CSB)**

What does Paul say, should our attitude to work be based on? Why?

⁹ **And masters, treat your slaves the same way, without threatening them, because you know that both their Master and yours is in heaven, and there is no favoritism with him. -- Ephesians 6:9 (CSB)**

What should slave masters be aware of?

Can you relate the slave/master relationship to contemporary society? How?

¹⁰ **Finally, be strengthened by the Lord and by his vast strength.** ¹¹ **Put on the full armor of God so that you can stand against the schemes of the devil.** ¹² **For our struggle is not against flesh and blood, but against the rulers, against the authorities, against the cosmic powers of this darkness, against evil, spiritual forces in the heavens. -- Ephesians 6:10-12 (CSB)**

Where should we draw our strength from?

Why should we put on the 'full armour of God'?

Who does Paul say, is our fight with?

---

[13] For this reason take up the full armor of God, so that you may be able to resist in the evil day, and having prepared everything, to take your stand. [14] Stand, therefore, with truth like a belt around your waist, righteousness like armor on your chest, [15] and your feet sandaled with readiness for the gospel of peace. [16] In every situation take up the shield of faith with which you can extinguish all the flaming arrows of the evil one. [17] Take the helmet of salvation and the sword of the Spirit — which is the word of God. [18] Pray at all times in the Spirit with every prayer and request, and stay alert with all perseverance and intercession for all the saints. -- Ephesians 6:13-18 (CSB)

List the armour of God and the purpose of each item.

What will the 'shield of faith' protect a believer from?

How can anyone pray at all times?

What does it mean to pray an intercessory prayer?

---

[19] Pray also for me, that the message may be given to me when I open my mouth to make known with boldness the mystery of the gospel. [20] For this I am an ambassador in chains. Pray that I might be bold enough to speak about it as I should. -- Ephesians 6:19-20 (CSB)

What is interesting to you about what Paul asks for in the prayers of others?

What does it mean to be an ambassador?

Do you think that you would consider yourself an ambassador? Why?

²¹ Tychicus, our dearly loved brother and faithful servant in the Lord, will tell you all the news about me so that you may be informed. -- Ephesians 6:21 (CSB)

Do you know of any missionaries? Write out a prayer for those who are on the mission field.

Interesting:

Tychicus is also mentioned in Acts 20:4, Colossians 4:7, 2 Timothy 4:12, and Titus 3:12.

---

²² I am sending him to you for this very reason, to let you know how we are and to encourage your hearts. ²³ Peace to the brothers and sisters, and love with faith, from God the Father and the Lord Jesus Christ. -- Ephesians 6:22-23 (CSB)

Why do you think, would the Ephesian Christians be encouraged by Paul's situation and letter?

24 Grace be with all who have undying love for our Lord Jesus Christ. -- Ephesians 6:24 (CSB)

Do you feel you have been blessed by God's grace? Why?

> **Prayer Suggestion:**
>
> Make a list of people that you would like to pray for. Pray for them to come to know the Lord Jesus Christ and be recipients of His grace.

Additional Study Question 1:

In verses 13-17 of chapter 6, we see the full armour of God. Write down how each piece of armour will protect you as a believer and how each item might motivate you to live a faithful life to glorify God.

Additional Study Question 2:

Write out a testimony of your Christian journey. Conclude with a prayer in which you thank God for His grace, the Lord Jesus Christ for His sacrifice and the Holy Spirit for His guidance.

Book of Ephesians, Chapter 6: Recap

What would you say is the main point Paul is trying to make in Chapter 6 of Ephesians?

Summarize the points that stand out most to you in this chapter of Ephesians.

How have these points made you reflect on your own life?

Summary: Book of Ephesians:

Ephesians show the position of the church in God's plan. It has always been a part of God plan. Today, God is building the church through His power and in the future, the church will reflect God's grace and wisdom.

The church must nurture unity within its ranks as it grows. It must act as a testimony to God. It must stand firm against God's enemy. The church relies on God and works with Him as it promotes unity among its genuine Christian members. It should set an example of holy living to the world; and as it stands against God's enemies using the equipment God has provided in the form of the armour of God.

In this letter, Paul highlights the supremacy of Christ. He gives information on both the nature of the church and on how church members should live. Besides, he stresses the unity of all believers—male, female, parent, child, master, slave— regardless of sex, nationality, or social rank. In the home and the church, living the Christian life can be difficult because we can't hide our imperfections from those who know us well. Close relationships between flawed people may lead to friction. On the other hand, these relationships may also lead to increased faith and deepened dependence on God. We can build unity in our churches through willing submission to Christ's leadership and heart-felt service to each another.

The church as God's spiritual organism, will be involved in a spiritual conflict. However, the power to engage the enemy is provided by God along with the weapons that Christians can use to protect themselves. The armour of God provide for the protection and resistance of the enemy. Covering every aspect of Christian life with prayer cements the fortitude Christians may draw from God.

Congratulations!

You have completed the study of the Book of Ephesians. Perhaps it was difficult, maybe not so tricky. In whatever way you worked through this study, I hope that you have learnt much.

> **Prayer Suggestion:**
>
> **Pray and ask God to help you apply what you have studied.**

Accepting Christ as your Saviour

Now. If you have not already done so, consider your relationship with the Lord Jesus Christ. Have you accepted Him as your Saviour? If not, consider the following aspect of Salvation:

Salvation is available for all!

Salvation is the most profound manifestation of God's love. The Salvation of sinners is not based on God overlooking sin. Sinners are saved by God, based on His moral foundation and because of the divine holiness of His character. This is known as Grace. It is based on God, so that human-kind cannot work for Salvation.

Acceptance of God's Salvation is profound, yet simple. It does not matter if one is wealthy, wise, educated or otherwise, nor does age, the colour of one's skin or any other difference matter. No one is turned away.

How do I become a Christian?

First, recognise that I am a sinner (Romans 3:23; 6:23; Ezekiel 18:4; John 5:24).

Secondly, realise that a relationship with Almighty God who is perfect, while I am not. This realisation requires that I rely on the Lord Jesus Christ as my Saviour, to make me acceptable in God's eyes (I Corinthians 15:3; 1 Peter 2:24; Isaiah 53:6; John 3:16).

Thirdly, exercising my free will, I accept the Lord Jesus Christ as my Saviour, believing that He perished on the Cross of Calvary for me, that through His completed work on that Cross, He has cleansed me of my sin (John 1:12; 3:36; Acts 16:31; 4:12).

The results of Salvation

My sins are removed from me (John 1:29),

I have eternal life (I John 5:11,12),

I am a new creation in Christ (2 Corinthians 5:17),

The Holy Spirit dwells within me (I Corinthians 6:19),

And I will never spiritually, perish (John 10:28-30).

Accepting Christ as your Saviour is life's most significant decision. This should be the goal of all people, aiming to achieve the point of our existence. I hope and pray anyone who has heard the Gospel and understood what it means, to become a Christian by trusting in the Lord Jesus Christ and be born again into God's eternal family (Matthew 11:28; John 1:12; Acts 4:12; 16:31).

Make the decision to accept Christ as your Saviour.

Finally,

The Grace of the Lord Jesus Christ, and the love of God, and the fellowship of the Holy Spirit be with you all. -- 2 Corinthians 13:13 (CSB)

Printed in Great Britain
by Amazon